MW01147801

the
Book of Crests

Scottish · American · clans

by
Mike McLaren

Published 1990 By

HERITAGE BOOKS, INC.
1540-E Pointer Ridge Place, Bowie, MD 20716
(301) 390-7709

ISBN 1-55613-401-0

A Complete Listing of Hundreds of Titles On
History, Genealogy, and Americana
Available Free Upon Request

ACKNOWLEDGEMENT

Naturally, to create a book of authentic Scottish crests such as this, a great deal of research was necessary, involving many ancient and modern tomes, before any of the artwork could even be imagined. Even after all the research and artwork had been completed, it was still necessary for it to be checked for authenticity by both Scottish and American heraldic authorities and clan societies.

My thanks go to the many individuals, clan societies and heraldic bodies of North America and Great Britain for their co-operation in providing much valuable information pertaining to the armorial crests contained herein.

Finally, but definitely not the lesser, are my thanks to my wife, Sue, for bearing with me without complaint as I worked on into many nights to complete the research and artwork. Thank you, Sue, for your patience and understanding.

MIKE

INTRODUCTION

As a heraldic artist, I have attempted to illustrate what I consider to be a full representation of badges bearing the crests and mottoes of the chiefs of major Scottish clans and names, past and present. I have also included the crest badges belonging to as many North American clan and family associations and societies as possible.

Along with each crest badge illustration, I have provided the blazon, the official description of the crest. The blazon is worded in the language of the herald, a language created from old Anglo/Norman-French with possibly a word or two borrowed from Middle Eastern tongues during the Holy Crusades. Each blazon describes the tinctures, the colours and metals, of its crest.

Included in the back of the book is a glossary where you will find definitions to the terminology that is used in the language of heraldic blazon. Due to the illustrations being printed in monochrome, I have used hatching, a system of lines and dots, to explain the colours in each crest wreath. These hatching patterns also are explained in the glossary.

My aim was to keep this collection of badges as accurate as possible at the time of publication, so I included crests of all the current chiefs of clans and names, as well as ancient crests. Many of the latter are dormant or even extinct, due to the chief-ship passing to another branch of the clan bearing a different crest or a chief passing without issue. All crests have been checked against Scottish records for authenticity; and where a chief recently adopted a new motto or crest, I have included only the new crest and motto here.

In order to publish the correct badges of the U.S. clan societies, I have enlisted the aid of as many of these societies as possible. In some cases, the crest or motto on the U.S. badge may vary from the crest and motto of the Scottish chief. Even the clan name may vary from the recognized Scottish clan name, e.g., clan Irvine becomes clan Irwin in the United States. Considering that these societies are officially recognized as the bodies representing the U.S. branches of Scottish clans, it would be wrong of me to include only the crest of the Scottish chief. So wherever a U.S. society has supplied me with details of its crest badge, I have accepted these details unchallenged and have drawn its badge as it was described by the clan.

I have used the same rule with mottoes. Most mottoes were adopted by clans many centuries ago, and in some cases, the Latin, French, Gaelic, et cetera, may not be spelled correctly. In these instances, if the clan's wishes are to keep the original spelling of the motto, I have presented it that way here.

Many books have been published over the past decades which pertain to clans, their histories, crests, and tartans. And each of these volumes contains a wealth of general information within its pages: colours and designs of tartans, Scottish maps, clan histories and the like. Therefore, I consider it unnecessary to repeat all the same information. My aim here, as an artist of armorial bearings and designs, is to render for the members of Scottish clans and names the correct designs of clan crests as laid down by heraldic law and ancient lore.

Primarily, this is a book of pictures, as it should be. After all, heraldic bearings (coats of arms) were originally created by men who could neither read nor write and needed some form of identification, a signature in symbols.

In Scotland, the coat of arms was, and still is, the display awarded to an individual of standing in his community (not just the chief of a clan or name) by the Lord Lyon, King of Arms, the official herald-in-chief for Scotland. The coat of arms is passed down or matriculated, usually through the heir male, the succeeding son, or at least through the direct blood line.

The *crest* is that part of the display which is attached to the top of the helmet, and usually resides above the *crest wreath* or *torse* (the ribbon of six twists, tinctured alternately of <1> the main metal [gold or silver], and <2> the main colour of the shield).

In many instances, the crest is blazoned as *issuing from a ducal* (or *crest) coronet*, or *on a cap of maintenance*, also called a *chapeau*. This style of device is always granted as a privilege of office or rank of nobility and, according to the laws of heraldry, only the grantee is permitted to display the crest upon either the coronet or the chapeau. Therefore, if it has been granted to the head of a clan, it should only be displayed by that individual; for it signifies that the clan chief is of high office or of noble birth. This rule only applies to either the ducal coronet or the chapeau.

In most instances throughout this book, whenever a crest is blazoned as resting upon either a coronet or a cap, I have drawn it as such. However, when a badge displaying the crest is used by a clansman, the coronet or the cap (whichever is drawn) should be deleted and replaced with a crest wreath, the ribbon of six twists.

The *crest badge* was originally worn by the members of a clan during battle or at gatherings, and when a clansman wore his chief's crest as a badge attached to his clothing with strap and buckle, he was making the statement, "I support my chief." He did not need to be literate, as he simply identified with his chief's *picture signature* and clan tartan.

Today, the crest and crest badge still have the same meaning as they did in days gone by. Only the chiefs have the right to bear their coats of arms and crests; but if clan members wish to show support for their chief or to declare their kinship with the clan, they may usually do so by displaying the crest badge -- the crest of the chief encircled by the fastened belt, the latter of which is inscribed with the motto of the chief.

You may notice that some of the mottoes have more than one translation, particularly when worded in Latin. For as much clarity as possible, I have added a second translation if I have thought it necessary. Where two or more names are mentioned on a badge, such as Anderson-MacAndrew, they are simply forms of the same name (both mean *son of Andrew*) and, therefore, belong to the same clan.

You may also notice that many of the pictures of beasts that are displayed here exhibit little, if any, resemblance to the creatures as we know them. One must always bear in mind that the ancient herald had probably never seen these creatures, so it was necessary for him to draw them according to fable, or the way he imagined they should appear. Because of this, a salamander may be portrayed looking more like a dragon, a dolphin may be brightly coloured with scales, a leopard may be a lion, and a lizard may be a wildcat.

Having explained this, I now invite you to peruse this book of Scottish and Scots-American clan badges.

Lang may yer lum reek,

vii

Mike McLaren, Heraldic Artist

THE ARTIST

Mike McLaren is a graphic artist who has studied as his specialty, the art and science of heraldry.

Although Mike was born and gained his early education in Great Britain, he obtained a major part of his schooling in Australia. His education included studies of the visual arts at the East Sydney College of Technical Arts and Sciences as well as broad overseas travel for practical studies. In his early years, he worked in different fields of art before focusing on this highly specialized field of armorial design.

He has travelled extensively throughout Britain, Europe, the Middle East, Australasia, and the United States, studying and researching the traditional heraldic styles of the individual cultures. These days, Mike has little use for many of those styles of heraldic art, but the knowledge of such subjects enhances the overall quality and value of his finished works.

Although a great deal of Mike's work is involved with the designing and reproduction of coat armor, his true specialization lies in the production of hand carved and painted armorial displays in wood. His commissions over the years have come from the ranks of nobility, city councils, corporations and individuals, all desirous of having their own coat of arms immortalized in wood, as coats of arms have traditionally been made for centuries. These commissions have also included such specialized heraldic works as totems and cigar store Indians.

The art associated with heraldry is not restricted to a country or a race. It exists in every culture on earth and always has existed, ever since man discovered the ability to create images with his mind; that faculty we know as imagination.

Mike now operates from his studio amid the serenity of the Blue Ridge mountains of North Carolina, where he lives with his American-born wife. Anybody wishing to contact him for further information should write to:

Mike McLaren
Route 4, Box 467
Boone, NC 28607

- Abercrombie of that Ilk -

Ancient Crest

Blazon -   *Out of a wreath of the liveries*
                 An oak tree acorned on a mount proper

Motto -   *Tace,* "Keep silence"

- Abercrombie of Birkenbog -

Chief's crest after 1636

Blazon -   *A falcon rising, belled proper*

Motto -   *Petit Alta,* "He seeks high things"
                    or "He aims at high things"

- Abernethy of that Ilk -

Ancient Crest

Blazon -   *A parrot feeding on a bunch of cherries proper*
           (Original crest--An eagle preparing to fly)

Motto -   *Salus per Christum,* "Salvation through Christ"

- Agnew -

Ancient and modern Crest

Blazon -   *An eagle issuant and reguardant proper*

Motto -   *Consilio non impetu,* **"By wisdom, not by rashness**

- Anderson - N███████ -

Crest of the ancient house of Airdbreck

U.S. Society - The Clan Anderson Society, Ltd.

Blazon -   *Out of a wreath of the liveries*
            An oak tree proper

Motto -   *Stand Sure,* "Stand your ground with confidence"

- ...ner of that Ilk -

Modern Crest

Blazon - *Two arms in armour holding a pole axe, with both hands gauntleted proper*

Motto - *Periissem ni periissem,* "I would have perished if I had not gone through to the end"

- Arbuthnott -

Ancient Crest

Blazon - *A peacock's head couped at the neck proper*

Motto - *Laus deo*, "Praise be to God"

- Armstrong -

Ancient house of Mangerton

U.S. Societies - The Armstrong Clan
and Armstrong Clan Society

Blazon -   *An arm embowed proper*

Motto -   *Invictus maneo*, "I remain unvanquished"
or "I remain unconquered"

- Baillie -

Ancient Crest

Blazon -   *A boar's head erased proper*

Motto -   *Quid clarius astris,* "What is brighter
          than the stars?"

- Bain -

Ancient Crest

Blazon -   *A dexter arm grasping a dirk proper*

Motto -   *Et marte et arte,* "Both by strength and art"

- Baird -

Crest of the ancient house of Auchmedden

U.S. Society - Baird Family Society Worldwide

Blazon -   *A griffin's head erased proper*

Motto -   *Dominus fecit,* "The Lord made"

- Balfour -

Ancient Crest

Blazon -   *A dexter arm in armour erect, the hand holding*
a baton in bend gules, tipped argent (often
drawn with the hand facing forward and baton in
bend sinister, but this is not true to blazon)

Motto -   *Fordward (from forthward),* "Forward"

- Barclay -

Ancient Barclay of that Ilk

U.S. Society - Clan Barclay Society

Blazon -   *Out of a chapeau azure turned ermine*
         A hand holding a dagger proper

Motto -   *Aut agere aut mori,* "Either to do or die"
           or "Either action or death"

- Beaton -

Ancient Clan Bethune

Blazon -   *An otter's head erased argent*

Motto -   *Debonnaire*, "Kindly" *or* "Gracious" (From old
French *de bon aire*, "of good disposition")

- Bell -

Crest of Clan Bell - in the U.S.A.

U.S. Society - The Bell Family Association of the
United States

Blazon -   *A hand holding a dagger proper*

Motto -   *I beir the bel,* "I bear the bell"

- Bell -

Crest of Clan Bell Descendants in the U.S.A.

Blazon - *A falcon close Or, hooded gules, belled and jessed proper*

Motto - *Nolite tradere, "Never give up"*

- Bisset of Lessendrum -

Ancient Crest

Blazon - *The trunk of an oak tree sprouting afresh proper*

Motto - *Abscissa virescit*, "Cut off, yet it blossoms"
or "Though lopped off, it flourishes"

- Blair -

Blazon -   A stag lodged proper

Motto -   *Amo probos,* "I love the virtuous"

- Borthwick of Borthwick -

Crest of the ancient Lords Borthwick

Blazon - *Out of a chapeau gules turned ermine*
A moor's head couped proper

Motto - *Qui conducit, "He who leads"*

- Borthwick of Borthwick -

Crest of the modern Chief

Blazon -   *A moor's head couped proper, wreathed about the temples with a torse argent and sable, the ribbons flotant*

Motto -   *Qui conducit,* "He who leads"

- Boyd -

Ancient and modern crest

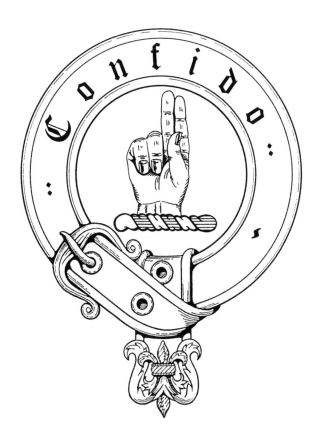

U.S. Society - House of Boyd Society

Blazon - *A dexter hand erect, pointing with the thumb and two fingers proper*

Motto - *Confido,* "I trust"

- Boyle of Kelburn -

Ancient and modern crest

Blazon - *An eagle displayed with two heads per pale embattled gules and argent*

Motto - *Dominus Providebit,* "The Lord will provide"

- Brodie of Brodie -

Ancient clan Brodie

Blazon -   *Out of a wreath of the liveries*
        A dexter hand holding a sheaf of arrows
        all proper

Motto -   *Unite,* "Come together"

- Broun of Colstoun -
(Scottish 'Brown')

Ancient Crest

Blazon - *A lion rampant holding in his dexter paw a fleur-de-lis, Or*

Motto - *Floreat Majestas*, "Let majesty flourish" or "Let greatness flourish"

- Bruce -

Ancient and modern crest

U.S. Societies - Family of Bruce Society in America and
Bruce International, U.S.A. Branch

Blazon -   *A lion statant, tail extended azure, armed
and langued gules*

Motto -   *Fuimus,* "We have been"

- Bruce -

Family of Bruce Society in America

(The crest of the founder of the U.S. society,
which is displayed to the sinister of the Chief's crest)

Blazon -   *A lion's head erased Or, langued gules*

Motto -   *Sum quid fui,* "I am what I was"

- Buchan -

Ancient Crest

Blazon -   *Out of a chapeau*
           The sun shining on a sunflower, full blown proper

Motto -   *Non inferiora secutus,* "Not having followed
           mean pursuits" *or* "Not following meaner things"

- Buchanan -

Ancient Crest

U.S. Society - Clan Buchanan Society in America, Inc.

Blazon -   *A hand holding up a ducal cap purpure lined ermine, tufted on the top with a rose gules within two branches of laurel, disposed orleways proper*

Motto -   *Clarior Hinc Honos,* "Hence the greater honour" *or* "Brighter hence the honour"

- Bullman -

Crest of the Family of Bullman Society
of North America

Blazon -   Out of a ducal coronet
            A bull's head proper

Motto -   Pro patria, "For my country"

- Burnett -

Crest of the modern Chief

U.S. Societies - Clan Burnett, Inc., The Burnett Society

Blazon -   *A cubit arm, the hand naked, vested vert doubled argent, pruning a vine tree with a pruning knife proper*

Motto -   *Virescit vulnere virtus,* "Virtue flourishes from a wound"

- Cameron -

Ancient and modern crest

U.S. Society - Clan Cameron U.S.A.

Blazon -   A sheaf of five arrows with points upwards,
             tied with a band gules

Motto -   Aonaibh ri cheile, "Unite"

- Campbell -

Ancient Crest

Blazon -   *Out of a wreath of the liveries*
              A boar's head couped Or

Motto -   *Ne obliviscaris, "Do not forget"*

- Campbell -

Crest of the Chief of Clan Campbell

U.S. Society - Clan Campbell Society, U.S.A.

Blazon -   *A boar's head fessewise, erased Or, armed*
           argent, langued gules

Motto -   *Ne obliviscaris,* "Forget not"

- Campbell of Cawdor -

Ancient Crest

Blazon -   *A swan proper, crowned Or*

Motto -   *Be mindful,* "Keep your mind on the job"
           (Second motto also used, *Candidus
           cantabit moriens,* "The pure soul will
           sing on its death-bed")

- Campbell of Breadalbane -

Ancient Crest

Blazon - *A boar's head erased proper*

Motto - Follow me

- Carmichael of Carmichael -

Ancient Crest

Blazon - *A dexter hand and arm in armour erect holding a broken spear proper*

Motto - *Toujours Prest,* "Always ready"

- Carnegie -

Crest of the modern Chief

Blazon -   *A thunderbolt proper, winged Or*

Motto -   *Dread God, "Beware the wrath of God"*

- Cathcart -

Crest of the Chief of Clan Cathcart

Blazon -   *A dexter hand couped above the wrist and erect*
proper, grasping a crescent argent as in the arms

Motto -   I hope to speed

- Charteris -

Crest of the modern Chief

Blazon -   *A dexter hand holding up a dagger paleways proper*

Motto -   *This is our charter,* "This is our sovereign right"

- Chattan -

Crest of The Clan Chattan Confederation

U.S. Society - Clan Chattan Confederation

Blazon -   *A cat salient proper*

Motto -   *Touch not the catt bot a glove,* "Be sure
                to wear gloves when you handle the cat"

- Cheyne -

Ancient Crest

Blazon -   *A cross pattee fitchee argent*

Motto -   *Patientia Vincit,* "He conquers by patience"

41

- Chisholm of Chisholm -

Crest of 'The Chisholm,' Chief of Clan Chisholm

Blazon -   *A dexter hand holding erect a dagger proper,*
            the point thereof transfixing a boar's head
            erased Or, armed proper, langued azure

Motto -   *Feros ferio,* "I strike the fierce" *or*
                        "I am fierce with the fierce"

42

- Cochrane -

Crest of the Chief of Clan Cochrane

U.S. Society - Clan Cochrane Society, U.S.A.

Blazon -   *A horse passant argent*

Motto -   *Virtute et labore,* "By virtue and labour"
or "By courage and labour"

- Cockburn -

Ancient Crest

Blazon -   *A cock crowing*

Motto -   *Accendit cantu,* "He rouses up by crowing"

- Colquhoun of Luss -

Crest of the Chief

Blazon -   *A hart's head couped gules, attired argent*

Motto -   *Si je puis,* "If I can"

- Colville -

Ancient Crest

Blazon - A hind's head couped at the neck, argent

Motto - Oublier ne puis, "I cannot forget"

- Craig -

Ancient Crest

Blazon - *A chevalier on horseback holding in his dexter hand a broken spear, all proper*

Motto - *J'ai bonne esperance*, "I have good hope" (Second motto also used is *Vive deo et vives*, "Live unto God and you will live")

- Cranstoun of that Ilk -

Crest of the modern Chief

Blazon - *A crane proper dormant holding a stone in her claw*

Motto - *Thou shalt want ere I want,*
        "You shall want before I do"

- Crawford -

Ancient Crest

Blazon - *A stag's head erased gules, between his attires a cross crosslet fitchee sable*

Motto - *Tutum te robore reddam,* "I will render you safe by my strength"

49

- Crichton of that Ilk -

Crest of the Chief

Blazon -   *A dragon spouting out fire proper*

Motto -   *God send grace, "God send compassion"*

- Cumming of Altyre -

Crest of the Chief

Blazon - *A lion rampant Or, in the dexter paw a dagger proper*

Motto - *Courage, "Fearlessness"*

- Cunning -

Ancient Crest

U.S. Society - Clan Cunning Association

Blazon -   *Out of a cap of maintenance gules turned ermine*
            A demi lion rampant of the first, armed and
            langued azure

Motto -   *Saorsa airson Albann,* "Freedom for Scotland"

- Cunningham -

Ancient crest as borne by
the Clan Cunningham Society of America

Blazon -   *A unicorn's head erased argent, armed and*
maned Or

Motto -   *Over fork over* (phrase from clan legend)

- Dalrymple -

Ancient Crest

Blazon - *A rock proper*

Motto - *Firm,* "Hard, like a rock"

- Dalzell -

Ancient Crest

U.S. Society - Clan Dalziel

Blazon -   A dagger erect azure, pommel and hilt Or

Motto -   I dare (translation of old Scottish *Dal zell*)

- Darroch of Gourock -

Crest of the Chief

Blazon - *A demi negro holding in the dexter hand a dagger proper*

Motto - Be watchful

- Davidson -

Ancient Crest

Blazon -   *A stag's head erased proper*

Motto -   *Sapienter si sincere,* "Wisely, if sincerely"

- Douglas -

Ancient Crest

U.S. Society - Clan Douglas Families/Septs

Blazon -   *On a chapeau gules furred ermine*
            A salamander vert in flames proper

Motto -Jamais arriere, "Never behind"

(As this is an ancient crest, I have used the ancient heraldic interpretation of the salamander--
A wingless dragon among flames. In *An Heraldic Alphabet,* J.P. Brooke-Little says that "In the
garter stall plate of James, ninth Earl of Douglas, who died in 1488, the salamander looks more
like a dog breathing flames.")

- Douglas -

Ancient Crest

Blazon -   (Modern interpretation of the salamander)
On a chapeau gules furred ermine
A salamander vert in flames proper

Motto -   Jamais Arriere, "Never behind"

- Drummond -

Crest of the Chief

U.S. Society - Clan Drummond Society of North America

Blazon -   *Out of a ducal coronet*
A goshawk, wings displayed proper,
armed and belled Or, jessed gules

Motto -   *Gang warily,* "Go with care"
(Second motto also used is *Virtutem coronat
honos* "Honour crowns virtue.")

- Dunbar of Mochrum -

Crest of the Chief

Blazon -   *A horse's head argent, bridled and reined gules*

Motto -   *In promptu,* "In readiness"

(The U.S. society uses the same crest badge, but it uses the motto *Sub spe,* "Under hope", as portrayed in the following crest.)

- Dunbar of the House of Dunbar -

Crest of society in the U.S.

Blazon -   *A horse's head argent, bridled and reined gules*

Motto -   *Sub spe*, "Under hope"

- Duncan of Ardounie -

Crest of senior Scottish Clan Duncan Family

U.S. Society - Clan Duncan Society

Blazon -   *A greyhound issuant proper, collared Or*

Motto -   *Vivat veritas,* "May truth flourish"

- Duncan -

Crest of the ancient chiefs
Duncan of Camperdown

U.S. Society - Clan Duncan Society

Blazon -   *A ship under sail*

Motto -   *Disce Pati,* "Learn to suffer" *or* "Learn to endure"

(This is the crest adopted by the American Clan Duncan Society)

- Dundas of Dundas -

Crest of the chief

Blazon - *A lion's head affrontee gules, looking through an oak bush, proper*

Motto - Essayez, "Try"

- Dunlop -

Crest of the Dunlop/Dunlap
Family Clan Society, Inc. in the U.S.A.

Blazon -   *A dexter hand holding a dagger erect,*
            all proper

Motto -   *Merito,* "Deservedly"

- Durie of Durie -

Crest of the Chief

Blazon -   *A crescent Or*

Motto -   *Confido*, "I trust"

- Eliott of Stobs -

Crest of the Chief

U.S. Society - Elliot Clan Society, U.S.A.

Blazon -   *A hand couped at the wrist in armour holding a cutlass in bend proper*

Motto -   *Fortiter et recte*, "Boldly and rightly"

(Many records depict the cutlass as a scimitar, but I have drawn it as it is blazoned.)

- Elphinstone -

Ancient Crest

Blazon - *A lady from the middle well attired proper,*
holding in her dexter hand a tower argent and
in her sinister a laurel branch proper

Motto - *Cause causit,* "Cause caused it to happen"

- Erskine -

Crest of the Chief

Blazon - *On a cap of maintenance gules, turned up ermine*
A dexter hand holding a skene in pale argent,
hilted and pommelled Or

Motto - *Je pense plus,* "I think more"

- Farquharson of Invercauld -

Crest of the Chief

Blazon - Out of a chapeau gules turned ermine
         A demi lion rampant gules, holding in the dexter
         paw a sword proper

Motto - Fide et fortitudine, "With faith and fortitude"

- Fergusson of Kilkerran -

Crest of the Chief

U.S. Society - Clan Ferguson Society of North America

Blazon -   *A bee on a thistle proper*

Motto -   *Dulcius ex asperis,* "Sweeter out of difficulties"

- Fleming -

Ancient Crest

Blazon -   *A goat's head erased argent, armed Or*

Motto -   *Let the deed shaw,* "Let the man
speak by his actions"

- Fletcher of Dunans -

Ancient Crest

U.S. Society - Clan Fletcher Society

Blazon -   *Two naked arms issuant proper, shooting*
              an arrow out of a bow sable

Motto -   *Recta Pete,* "Seek what is right"

(The U.S. Clan Fletcher Society uses the same crest badge, but
it has adopted *Alta Pete,* "Aim at high things" for its motto.)

- Forbes of Forbes -

Crest of the chief

Blazon -   *Out of a wreath of the liveries*
   A stag's head attired with ten tynes proper

Motto -   *Grace me guide, "Let grace be my guide"*

- Forrester -

Ancient Crest
Crest of the U.S. Clan Forrester Society

Blazon - *A ratchhound's head erased Or, collared gules*

Motto - *Blaw hunter, blaw thy horn,* "Blow hunter, blow your horn"

- Forsyth of that Ilk -

Ancient and modern Crest

U.S. Society - Clan Forsyth of America, Inc.

Blazon -   *A griffin segreant azure, armed and membered sable, crowned Or*

Motto -   *Instaurator ruinæ*, "Repairer of ruin"

- Fotheringham -

Ancient Crest

Blazon - *A griffin segreant proper*

Motto - *Be it fast,* "Let it be fast"

- Fraser -

Ancient Crest of the Lords Saltoun

Blazon - *An ostrich with a horseshoe in its beak, all proper*

Motto - In God is all

- Fraser -

Crest of the Chief of the name, Fraser

U.S. Societies - Clan Fraser Society of North America
and Clan Fraser Associates, Inc.

Blazon -   *On a mount, a flourish of strawberries,*
             leaved and fructed proper

Motto -   All my hope is in God

- Fraser of Lovat -

Chief of Clan Fraser of Lovat

Blazon -   *A buck's head erased proper*

Motto -   *Je suis prest, "I am ready"*

- Fraser of Muchalls -

Ancient Crest

Blazon -   *A bunch of strawberries proper*

Motto -   All my hope is in God

- Fullarton of that Ilk -

Ancient Crest

Blazon -   *A camel's head and neck erased proper*

Motto -   *Lux in tenebris, "Light in darkness"*

- Gair of Nigg -

Ancient Crest

Blazon -   A mill-rind

Motto -   Sero sed serio, "Slow but sure"

- Gayre of Gayre and Nigg -

Crest of the chief

Blazon -   *Issuant from a crest coronet Or*
                A mount vert

Motto -   *Sero sed serio,* "Slow but sure"

- Galbreath (Galbraith) -

Ancient Crest

Blazon -   *A bear's head couped argent,*
            muzzled azure

Motto -   *Ab obice suavior,* "More smooth
            from an obstacle"

- Gardyne -

Ancient Crest

Blazon -   *Two dexter hands couped and conjoined*
           in fesse, supporting a cross-crosslet
           fitchee Or

Motto -   *Cruciata cruce junguntur,* "Afflictions
           are connected with the cross"

87

- Gillespie of Newton -

Ancient Crest

Blazon -   *An anchor proper*

Motto -   *Tu certa salutis anchora,* "Thou a
sure anchor of salvation"

- Gordon -

Crest of the Chief

U.S. Society - House of Gordon, U.S. branch

Blazon -   *Issuing from a ducal coronet Or*
                A hart's head and neck affrontee proper,
                attired with ten tynes of the first

Motto -   *Bydand,* "Remaining"

- Graham -

Crest of the Chief

U.S. Society - Clan Graham Society

Blazon -   *A falcon proper, beaked and armed Or,*
            killing a stork argent, armed gules

Motto -   *N'oubliez, "Forget not"*

- Grant -

Crest of the Chief

U.S. Society - Clan Grant Society of North America, Inc.

Blazon -   *A burning hill proper*

Motto -   *Craig elachie,* "The rock of alarm"

(The U.S. Clan Grant Society uses the same badge as the Scottish Chief, but it uses the ancient motto, *"Stand fast"*, which is now borne below the shield of the Scottish Chief.)

- Gray -

Ancient Crest

Blazon -   *An anchor in pale Or*

Motto -   *Anchor, fast anchor,* "Hold fast anchor, don't let go"

- Grierson of Lagg -

Ancient Crest

Blazon -   *A fetterlock argent*

Motto -   *Hoc securior,* "Safer by this"

- Gunn -

Ancient Crest

U.S. Society - Clan Gunn Society of North America

Blazon -   *A dexter hand wielding a sword proper*

Motto -   *Aut pax aut bellum*, "Either peace or war"

- Guthrie of that Ilk -

Ancient Crest

U.S. Society - Clan Guthrie, U.S.A., Inc.

Blazon -   *A dexter arm holding a drawn sword proper*

Motto -   *Sto pro veritate,* "I stand for truth"

- Haig -

Crest of the Chief

Blazon -   *A rock proper*

Motto -   *Tyde what may,* "What will be, will be"

- Haldane of Gleneagles -

Ancient and modern Crest

Blazon -   *An eagle's head erased Or*

Motto -   **Suffer**

- Hamilton -

Ancient Crest

U.S. Society - Clan Hamilton Society

Blazon -   *On a ducal coronet, an oak tree, fructed and penetrated transversely in the main stem by a frame saw proper, the frame Or*

Motto -   **Through**

- Hannay of that Ilk -

Ancient and modern crest

Blazon -   *A cross-crosslet fitchee, issuing*
             out of a crescent sable

Motto -   *Per ardua ad alta,* "Through
                   difficulties to heights"

- Hay -

Crest of the Chief

U.S. Society - Clan Hay

Blazon -   Out of a ducal coronet
A falcon volant proper, armed, jessed
and belled Or

Motto -   Serva jugum, "Keep the yoke"
("Keep the bond" *or* "Keep the union")

- Henderson of Fordell -

Crest of the Chief

U.S. Society - Clan Henderson Society

Blazon -   A cubit arm proper, the hand holding an
estoile Or and surmounted by a crescent azure

Motto -   Sola virtus nobilitat, "Virtue alone ennobles"

- Hepburn -

Ancient Crest

Blazon - *A horse furnished gules and tied to a tree proper*

Motto - *Keep traist*

(In medieval English, "Keep trust" or "keep the faith")

- Hepburn -

Crest of the U.S. Hepburn Family Association

U.S. Society - Hepburn Family Association

Blazon -   *A horse's head couped proper, garnished gules*

Motto -   Keep Trust

- Home of the Hirsel-

Ancient Crest

Blazon -   *On a cap of maintenance proper,*
a lion's head erased argent, armed
and langued gules

Motto -   A home, a home, a home

- Hope of Craighall -

Ancient Crest

Blazon -   *A broken globe surmounted of a rainbow proper*

Motto -   *At spes infracta,* "Yet my hope is not broken"

- Hunter of Hunterston -

Crest of the Chief

U.S. Society - The Hunter Clan Association

Blazon - *A greyhound sejant proper, gorged with an*
           antique crown Or

Motto - *Cursum perficio,* "I accomplish my course"

- Innes -

Ancient Crest

U.S. Society - Innes Clan Society

Blazon -   *A boar's head erased proper, langued gules*

Motto -   *Be traist, "Be faithful"*

- Irvine of Drum -

Crest of the Chief

Blazon - *A sheaf of nine holly leaves vert, slipped and banded gules*

Motto - *Sub sole sub umbra virens,* "Flourishing both in sunshine and in shade"

(The U.S. branch of Clan Irvine (called Clan Irwin) recognizes both the crest of the Chief, as it appears above, and also the crest that is displayed on the following page.)

- Irvine of Bonshaw -

The Crest of the U.S. Clan Irwin Association

Blazon -   *An arm gauntleted, the hand holding a branch*
            of holly consisting of seven leaves proper

Motto -   *Haud ullis labentia ventis, "Yielding*
                    under no winds"

- Jardine of Applegirth -

Crest of the Chief

U.S. Society - The Jardine Clan Society
of Southern California

Blazon -   *A spur-rowel of six points proper*

Motto -   *Cave, adsum,* "Beware, I am present"

- Johnstone of Annandale -

Crest of the Chief

U.S. Society - Clan Johnston(e) in America

Blazon -   A winged spur erect Or

Motto -   *Nunquam non paratus,* "Never unprepared"

- Keith -

Crest of the Chief

U.S. Society - Clan Keith

Blazon -   *Out of a crest coronet*
         A roebuck's head proper, attired Or

Motto -   *Veritas vincit,* "Truth conquers"

- Kennedy -

Crest of the Chief

Blazon -   *A dolphin naiant, proper*

Motto -   *Avise la fin,* "Consider the end"

- Kerr -

Crest of the Chief

Blazon -   *A sun in splendour Or*

Motto -   *Sero sed serio, "Late, but in earnest"*

- Kincaid of Kincaid -

Crest of the Chief

U.S. Society - Clan Kincaid International

Blazon - A triple towered castle argent, masoned sable, and issuing from the centre tower a dexter arm from the shoulder embowed, vested in the proper tartan and grasping a drawn sword all proper

Motto - This I'll defend

(The U.S. Society's motto is "I will defend.")

115

- Kirkpatrick -

Ancient Crest

Blazon -   *A hand holding a dagger in pale distilling drops of blood*

Motto -   I make sure

- Lamont of that Ilk -

Crest of the Chief

Blazon -   *A dexter hand open paleways,
couped at the wrist proper*

Motto -   Ne parcas nec spernas, "Neither
spare nor despise"

- Lauder of Bass -

Ancient Crest

Blazon -   *A solan goose sitting on a rock proper*

Motto -   *Sub umbra alarum tuarum,* "Under the
                          shadow of thy wings"

- Leask of Leask -

Crest of the Chief

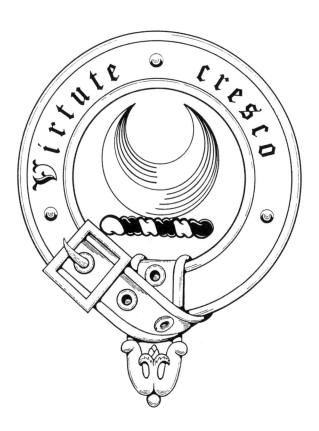

Blazon -   *A crescent argent*

Motto -   *Virtute cresco,* "I increase by virtue"

- Lennox of that Ilk -

Crest of the Chief

Blazon -   *Two broadswords in saltire behind*
            a swan's head and neck, all proper

Motto -   I'll defend

- Leslie -

Crest of the Chief

U.S. Society - American Clan Leslie Society

Blazon -   *Out of a wreath of the liveries*
              A demi-griffin proper, armed and winged Or

Motto -   *Grip fast,* **"Hang on with determination"**

- Lindsay -

Crest of the Chief

U.S. Society - Clan Lindsay Association USA, Inc.

Blazon -   *Out of an antique ducal coronet*
             A swan's head, neck and wings proper

Motto -   Endure fort, "Endure with strength"

- Livingston(e) -

Ancient Crest

Blazon - *A demi-hercules, wreathed about the head and middle, holding in the dexter hand a club erect, and in the sinister a serpent all proper*

Motto - *Si je puis,* "If I can"

- Lockhart of the Lee -

Crest of the Chief

Blazon -   *A boar's head erased argent, langued gules*

Motto -   *Corda serrata pando,* "I lay open a heart
locked up"

- Logan of that Ilk -

Ancient Crest

Blazon - *A passion nail piercing a man's heart proper*

Motto - *Hoc majorum virtus,* "This is the valour of my ancestors"

- Lumsden of that Ilk -

Ancient Crest

U.S. Society - Clan Lumsden Association of North America

Blazon -   *An earn or hawk feeding on a salmon proper*

Motto -   Beware in time (or tyme)

126

- Lumsden of that Ilk -

Crest of the Chief

U.S. Society - Clan Lumsden Association of North America

Blazon -   *A naked arm grasping a sword proper*

Motto -   *Amor patitur moras,* "Love endures delay"

The U.S. Society uses the motto "Dei Dono sum quod sum", (By the bounty of God I am what I am)

- Lyle -

Ancient Crest

Blazon -   *A cock Or, crested gules*

Motto -   *An I may,* "If I may"

128

- Lyon -

Ancient Crest

Blazon -   *A lady from the middle richly attired,*
holding in her dexter hand a thistle,
within a garland of bay leaves all proper

Motto -   *In te domine speravi,* "In thee, oh Lord,
have I put my trust"

- MacAlister -

Ancient Crest

Blazon -   *A dexter hand holding a dirk in pale, both proper*

Motto -   Fortiter, "Bravely"

130

- MacAlpin -

Ancient Crest
Crest of the Clan MacAlpin Association of North America

Blazon -   *A saracen's head, couped at the neck and*
           distilling drops of blood, all proper

Motto -   *Cuinich bas Alpin,* "Remember the
              death of Alpin"

- MacArthur -

Ancient Crest

U.S. Society - Clan MacArthur Society, Inc.

Blazon -   *Two laurel branches in orle, proper*

Motto -   *Fide et opera,* "By fidelity and labour"

132

- MacAulay -

Ancient Crest

Blazon -   A boot couped at the ankle, thereon a spur,
all proper

Motto -   Dulce Periculum, "Danger is sweet"

- MacBean (MacBain) -

Crest of the Chief

U.S. Society - Clan McBean in North America, Inc.

Blazon -   *A grey demi cat-a-mountain salient, on his*
           sinister foreleg a highland targe gules

Motto -   *Touch not a catt bot a targe,* "Don't attempt
           to touch a cat, without a shield"

134

- MacBeth -

*Crest as borne by the Clan MacBeth Society
of North America*

Blazon -   *A wyvern holding in the dexter claw a sword in
            pale proper, the hilt entwined with two serpents
            argent and vert*

Motto -   *Conjuncta virtuti fortuna,* "Fortune is
            allied to bravery"

- MacCallum -

Ancient Crest

U.S. Society - Clan MacCallum-Malcolm Society

Blazon -   *A tower argent, window and port azure*

Motto -   *In ardua tendit,* "He attempts
                          difficult things"

- MacCorquodale -

Ancient Crest

Blazon - *A stag standing at gaze proper, attired gules*

Motto - *Vivat Rex,* **"Long life to the King"**

- MacCubbin -

Ancient Crest
As borne by the Clan McCubbin Society of North America

Blazon - *An arm in armour embowed, grasping a scimitar*

Motto - *Pro rege et patria,* "For king and country"

- MacCulloch -

Ancient Crest

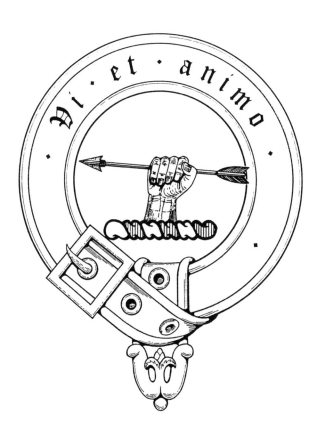

Blazon - *A hand throwing a dart proper*

Motto - *Vi et animo,* **"By strength and courage"**

139

- MacDonald of MacDonald -

Crest of the Chief

U.S. Society - Clan Donald, U.S.A., Inc.

Blazon -   Out of a coronet
A hand in armour fesseways couped at the elbow
proper, holding a cross-crosslet fitchee gules

Motto -   Per mare per terras, "By sea, by lands"

- MacDonald of Clanranald -

Crest of the Chief
of the House of Clanranald

Blazon -   Out of a wreath of the liveries
            A castle triple towered argent, masoned
            sable, and issuing from the centre tower
            a dexter arm in armour embowed, grasping
            a sword, all proper

Motto -   My hope is constant in thee

- MacDonald of Sleat -

Chief of Clan Husteain

Blazon -   Out of a wreath of the liveries
              A dexter hand in armour fessewise,
              holding a cross-crosslet fitchee gules

Motto -   Per mare per terras, "By sea, by lands"

- MacDonald -

Ancient Lords of the Isles

Blazon -   *A raven sable standing on a rock azure*

Motto -   *Fraoch eilean, "Heathery isle"*

- MacDonell of Glengarry -

Crest of the Chief

Blazon - *A raven proper, perched on a rock azure*

Motto - *Cragan an fhithich,* "The rock of the raven"

- MacDougall of MacDougall -

Crest of the Chief

U.S. Society - Clan MacDougall Society of the
United States and Canada

Blazon -   *On a cap of maintenance, a dexter arm in armour
embowed fesseways couped proper, holding a cross-
crosslet fitchee erect gules*

Motto -   *Buaidh no bas,* "Victory or death"

- MacDowall of Garthland -

Crest of the Chief
MacDowell of Garthland

Blazon - *A lion's paw erased and erect, and holding a dagger point upwards proper, pommelled and hilted Or*

Motto - *Vincere vel mori, "To conquer or die"*

- MacDuff -

Ancient Crest

U.S. Society - Clan MacDuff Society of America, Inc.

Blazon -   *A demi-lion rampant gules holding in*
             the dexter paw a broadsword proper,
             hilted and pommelled Or

Motto -   *Deus juvat,* "God assists"

- MacEwen -

Ancient Crest

U.S. Society - Clan MacEwan Association of North America

Blazon - *The trunk of an oak tree with a branch sprouting forth on either side*

Motto - *Reviresco, "I flourish again"*

- MacFaddien -

Crest of the
MacFaddien Family Society

Blazon -   *A dexter arm in armour embowed, wielding a sword proper*

Motto -   *Lamh laidir an nachtar,* "The strong hand uppermost"

- MacFarlane of that Ilk -

Ancient Crest

U.S. Society - Clan MacFarlane Society.

Blazon -   *A demi-savage brandishing in his dexter hand a broadsword proper and pointing with the sinister to an imperial crown Or*

Motto -   This I'll defend

- MacFie of Dreghorn -

Ancient Crest

U.S. Society - MacFie Clan Society of North America

Blazon - *A demi-lion rampant proper*

Motto - *Pro Rege,* "For the King"

- MacGillivray -

Ancient Crest

Blazon - *A stag's head couped proper, tyned Or*

Motto - *Dunmaglas* (the name of their homeland)

152

- MacGillivray -

*Crest of the most senior modern
MacGillivray Family*

Blazon -   A cat-a-mountain sejant guardant proper,
his dexter forepaw in a guardant posture
and his tail reflexed under his sinister paw

Motto -   Touch not this cat, "Beware when you
approach this cat"

- MacGregor of MacGregor -

Crest of the Chief

Blazon - *A lion's head erased proper, crowned with an antique crown Or*

Motto - *S'rioghal mo dhream,* "Royal is my race"

- MacIain -

Ancient Crest -

Blazon - *A demi-eagle displayed sable*

Motto - *In hope I byde, "In hope I remain"*
or "I wait in hope"

- MacInnes -

Ancient Crest

U.S. Society - Clan MacInnes Society

Blazon -   *A bee sucking a thistle proper*

Motto -   *E labore dulcedo,* "Pleasure arises
out of labour"

- MacIntyre of Glenoe -

Ancient Crest

U.S. Society - Clan MacIntyre Association

Blazon -   *A dexter hand holding a dagger in pale,*
             both proper

Motto -   *Per ardua,* "Through difficulties"

- MacIver of Asknish -

Ancient Crest

Blazon - *A boar's head couped Or*

Motto - *Nunquam obliviscar, "I will never forget"*

- MacKay -

Crest of the Chief

U.S. Societies - Clan MacKay Society of North America and Clan MacKay Society of North America/Pacific Coast, Inc.

Blazon -   *A dexter arm erect, couped at the elbow, the hand grasping a dagger, also erect proper*

Motto -   *Manu forti,* "With a strong hand"

- MacKellar -

Ancient Crest

Blazon - *An arm in armour embowed, wielding a scimitar proper*

Motto - *Perseverando,* "By persevering"

- MacKenzie -

Crest of the Chief

U.S. Society - Clan MacKenzie Society in the Americas, Inc.

Blazon - *A mount in flames proper*

Motto - *Luceo non uro,* "I shine, not burn"

- MacKie -

Ancient Crest

Blazon - *A raven proper*

Motto - *Labora,* "By labour"

- MacKindlay -

Ancient Crest

Blazon -   *An eagle's head erased proper*

Motto -   *Spernit humum,* "He despises the earth"

- MacKinnon of MacKinnon -

Crest of the Chief

U.S. Society - The Clan MacKinnon Society
of North America

Blazon - *A boar's head erased, holding in the mouth
the shinbone of a deer, all proper*

Motto - *Audentes fortuna juvat,* "Fortune assists the daring"

- MacKintosh of MacKintosh -

Crest of the Chief

U.S. Society - Clan MacKintosh of North America

Blazon -   *A cat-a-mountain salient guardant proper*

Motto -   *Touch not the cat bot a glove,* "Do not
approach the cat without gloves"

165

- MacLachlan of MacLachlan -

Crest of the Chief

U.S. Society - Clan MacLachlan Association (N.A.)

Blazon -   Out of a crest coronet
           A castle set upon a rock, all proper

Motto -   Fortis et fidus, "Brave and faithful"

- MacLaine of Lochbuie -

Ancient Crest

U.S. Societies - Clan MacLaine of Lochbuie
and Clan Gillean Association

Blazon -   *A branch of laurel and of cypress in saltire,
surmounted of a battle-axe in pale, all proper*

Motto -   *Vincere vel mori*, "To conquer or die"

- MacLaren of MacLaren -

Crest of the Chief

U.S. Society - Clan MacLaren Society of North America, Ltd.

Blazon -   *On a wreath of the liveries*
              A lion's head erased sable, crowned with an antique
              crown of six (four visible) points Or, between two
              branches of laurel issuing from the wreath at either
              side of the head, both proper

Motto -   *Creag an tuirc,* "The boar's rock"

- MacLean -

Crest of the Chief

U.S. Societies - Clan MacLean Association -
Pacific Coast Branch, and Clan Gillean Association.

Blazon -   *A tower embattled argent*

Motto -   *Virtue mine honour,* "Virtue is my distinction"

- MacLellan -

Ancient Crest

U.S. Society - Clan MacLellan in America, Inc.

Blazon -   *A naked arm supporting on the point of a sword,*
                a moor's head

Motto -   Think on

- MacLennan of MacLennan -

Crest of the Chief

U.S. Society - Clan MacLennan Association

Blazon -   *A demi-piper all proper, garbed in the proper tartan of the Clan MacLennan*

Motto -   *Dum spiro spero,* "While I breathe, I hope"

- MacLeod of MacLeod -

Crest of the Chief

U.S. Society - Clan MacLeod Society U.S.A., Inc.

Blazon -   *A bull's head cabossed sable, horned Or, between two flags gules, staves sable*

Motto -   *Hold fast, "Stand your ground"*

- MacLeod of the Lewes -

Ancient Lords of Lewis

Blazon -   *The sun in his splendour Or*

Motto -   *I birn quhil I se* (ancient Scottish)
"I burn while I shall"
(Sometimes recorded as *I burn weil, I see*)

- MacMillan of MacMillan -

Crest of the Chief

U.S. Society - Clan MacMillan Society of North America

Blazon -   *A dexter and a sinister hand issuant, grasping and brandishing a two-handed sword proper*

Motto -   *Miseris succurrere disco,* "I learn to succour the distressed"

174

- MacNab of MacNab -

Crest of the Chief

U.S. Society - The Clan MacNab Society of North America

Blazon -   *A savage's head affronte, erased proper*

Motto -   *Timor omnis abesto,* "Let all fear be absent"

- MacNaghten of MacNaghten -
- and Dundarave -

Crest of the Chief

Blazon -   *A tower embattled gules*

Motto -   I hope in God

- MacNeacail of MacNeacail -
- and Scorrybreac -
(MacNicol)

Crest of the Chief

Blazon -   *A hawk's head erased gules*

Motto -   *Sgorra bhreac*

(Scorrybreac is the name of the Scottish homeland
of the MacNeacail Clan.)

- MacNeil of Barra -

Crest of the Chief

U.S. Society - Clan MacNeil Association of America

Blazon -   *A rock proper*

Motto -   *Buaidh no bas,* "Victory or death"

   (The U.S. society uses *"Vincere vel mori"*,
   "To conquer or die", for its motto)

- MacPherson of Cluny -

Crest of the Chief

Touch not the cat but a glove

U.S. Societies - Clan MacPherson Association,
United States Branch

Blazon -   *Out of a wreath of the liveries*
            A cat sejant proper

Motto -   *Touch not the cat but a glove,* "Do not
            approach the cat without gloves"

(Although not blazoned as such, the herald's drawing
shows the cat with its sinister paw raised, as above.)

- MacQuarrie -
- MacGuarie of Ulva -

Ancient Crest

Blazon -   *Out of an antique crown*
An arm in armour embowed, grasping a
dagger all proper

Motto -   *Turris fortis mihi deus,* **"God is a**
strong tower to me"

- MacQueen of Corrybrough -

Ancient Crest

Blazon -   *An heraldic tiger rampant ermine holding an
arrow, point downwards argent, pheoned gules*

Motto -   Constant and faithful

- MacQueen of Corrybrough -

Ancient Crest

Blazon -   *A wolf rampant ermine, supporting an*
            arrow, point downwards argent, pheoned gules

Motto -   Constant and faithful

(Some records show this badge to be a wolf instead of
an heraldic tiger, as portrayed in the previous crest,
so I have drawn both badges.)

- MacRae -

Ancient Crest

U.S. Society - Clan MacRae Society of North America

Blazon -   *A mailed arm embowed, the hand grasping*
                  a Turkish scimitar proper

Motto -   *Fortitudine,* "With fortitude"

- MacThomas of Finegand -

Crest of the Chief

Blazon -   *A demi cat-a-mountain rampant guardant proper,*
           grasping in his dexter paw a serpent vert, langued
           gules, its tail environing the sinister paw

Motto -   *Deo juvante invidiam superabo,* "With God's
                      help, I shall conquer envy"

- Maitland -

Crest of the Chief

U.S. Society - Clan Maitland Society of North America

Blazon -   *A lion sejant affrontee gules, ducally crowned*
              proper, in his dexter paw a sword of the last,
              hilted and pommelled Or, and in his sinister a
              fleur-de-lis azure

Motto -   *Consilio et animis,* "By wisdom and courage"

- Makgill -

Crest of the Chief

U.S. Society - MacGill Society U.S.A.

Blazon -   *A phoenix in flames proper*

Motto -   *Sine fine,* "Without end"

- Malcolm of Poltalloch -

Crest of the Chief

U.S. Society - Clan MacCallum-Malcolm Society

Blazon -   *A tower argent*

Motto -   *In ardua petit,* "He aims at difficult things"

- Mar(r) -

Crest of the Chief

Blazon -   Upon a chapeau gules faced ermine
Two wings each of ten pen feathers, erected and
addorsed, both blazoned as the shield: azure a
bend between six cross-crosslets fitchee Or

Motto -   Pans plus, "Think more"

- Marjoribanks of that Ilk -

Crest of the Chief

Blazon -   *A demi-griffin proper*

Motto -   *Et custos et pugnax,* "Both a
                    preserver and a champion"

- Matheson of Matheson -

Crest of the Chief

Blazon -   *Issuing from an eastern crown Or*
             A hand brandishing a scimitar in fesse proper

Motto -   *Fac et spera,* "Do and hope"

- Maule of Panmure -

Ancient Crest

Blazon - *A dragon vert spouting out fire*
at mouth and tail

Motto - *Clementia tecta rigore, "Clemency*
concealed under rigour"

- Maxtone of Cultoquhey -

Ancient Crest

Blazon -   *A bee volant proper*

Motto -   *Providus esto,* "Be cautious"

192

- Maxwell -

Ancient Crest

U.S. Society - Clan Maxwell Society of the U.S.A.

Blazon -   *A stag proper, attired argent, lodged*
             before a holly bush, also proper

Motto -   *Reviresco, "I flourish again"*

- Melville of Melville -

Ancient Crest

Blazon -   *A ratch-hound's head erased proper,*
           collared gules

Motto -   *Denique Cœlum,* "Heaven at last"

- Menzies of Menzies -

Crest of the Chief

U.S. Society - Clan Menzies Society

Blazon -   *On a wreath of his liveries*
             A saracen's head erased, wreathed proper

Motto -   *Vil God I zal,* "Will God I shall"

- Moffat of that Ilk -

Crest of the Chief

U.S. Society - Moffat Clan Society of North America

Blazon -   *A crest coronet and issuing therefrom*
A cross-crosslet fitchee sable surmounted of a
saltire argent

Motto -   *Spero meliora,* "I hope for better things"

- Moncreiffe of that Ilk -

Ancient Crest

Blazon -   Out of a crest coronet Or
           A demi-lion rampant gules, armed and langued azure

Motto -   Sur esperance, "Upon hope"

- Montgomerie -

Crest of the Chief

U.S. Society - Clan Montgomery Society of North America, Inc.

Blazon - *A lady dressed in ancient apparel azure, holding in her dexter hand an anchor Or, and in her sinister the head of a savage couped, suspended by the hair, all proper*

Motto - *Garde bien,* "Guard well"

- Morrison -

Crest of the Chief

U.S. Society - Clan Morison of North America

Blazon -   *Issuant from waves of the sea azure crested argent, a mount vert, thereon an embattled wall azure masoned argent, and issuant therefrom a cubit arm naked proper, the hand grasping a dagger azure hilted Or*

Motto -   *Teaghlach Phabbay*, "Family of Phabbay"

- Mowat -

Ancient Crest

U.S. Society - Mowat Family International

Blazon -   *The battlement of a castle Or, issuant therefrom*
a demi-warrior, armed and accoutred proper, holding
in his dexter hand a sword also proper, hilted and
pommelled Or, and in his sinister a flagstaff,
thereon hoisted a banner vert, fringed and charged
with an antique crown Or

Motto -   *Monte alto,* "On a high mount"

- Muir -

Ancient Crest

Blazon -   *A savage's head couped proper*

Motto -   *Durum patentia frango,* "I overcome
                    difficulty by patience"

201

- Munro of Foulis -

Crest of the Chief

U.S. Society - Clan Munro Association

Blazon -   *An eagle perching proper*

Motto -   *Dread God, "Fear God"*

- Murray -

Crest of the Chief

U.S. Society - The Murray Clan Society

Blazon -   *A mermaid holding in her dexter hand a*
             mirror, and in her sinister a comb, all proper

Motto -   *Tout prest, "Quite ready"*

- Napier of Napier -

Ancient Crest

U. S. Society - Clan Napier in North America

Blazon -   *A dexter arm from the elbow in pale proper, grasping a crescent argent*

Motto -   *Sans tache,* "Without stain"

- Nicolson -

Crest of the Chief

Blazon - *A lion issuant Or, armed and langued gules*

Motto - *Generositate, "By generosity"*

205

- Nisbet of that Ilk -

Ancient Crest

U.S. Society - Nesbitt/Nisbet Society of North America

Blazon -   *A boar passant sable*

Motto -   *I byde it* (or *I byd it*), "I command it"

206

- Ogilvy -

Crest of the Chief

Blazon - *A lady affrontee from the middle upwards proper in azure vestments richly attired, holding a portcullis gules*

Motto - *A fin,* "To the end"

- Oliphant -

Ancient Crest

Blazon -   A unicorn's head couped argent,
           maned and horned Or

Motto -   A tout pourvoir, "To provide for all"

208

- Paisley -

Badge of the
Paisley and Allied Families Society

(There is no blazon for this badge because it is not a heraldic crest, but as it is the identifying badge of a Clan Society, I have included it in this collection.

- Pollock -

Ancient Crest -

U.S. Society - Clan Pollock (Cinneadh Pollag)

Blazon -   *A boar passant shot through with a dart proper*

Motto -   *Audacter et strenue,* "Boldly and earnestly"

- Preston of that Ilk -

Ancient Crest

Blazon -   *A good angel proper*

Motto -   *Præsto ut Præstem,* "I undertake that
I may perform"

- Pringle of Torsonce -

Ancient Crest

U.S. Society - Clan Pringle

Blazon -   *An escallop Or*

Motto -   *Amicitia reddit honores,* "Friendship
gives honours"

- Ramsay -

Crest of the Chief

U.S. Society - Clan Ramsay Association
of North America

Blazon -　　*A unicorn's head, couped at the neck argent,
armed, maned and tufted Or*

Motto -　　*Ora et Labora, "Pray and Labour"*

- Rattray of Rattray -

Crest of the Chief

Blazon - *Out of a crest coronet*
A star Or, and thereon a flaming heart proper

Motto - *Super sidera votum,* "My desires extend
beyond the stars"

- Robertson of Struan -

Crest of the Chief

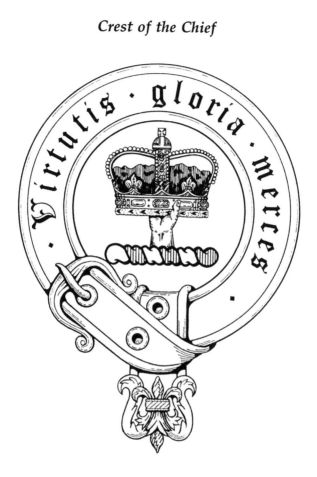

U.S. Societies - Clan Donnachaidh Society,
the Clan Donnachaidh Society of California, Inc.,
and Clan Donnachaidh Society of New England

Blazon -   *A dexter hand erect, holding an imperial*
           crown all proper

Motto -   *Virtutis gloria merces,* "Glory is the
                      reward of valour"

- Rollo -

Crest of the Chief

Blazon -   *A stag's head couped at the neck proper*

Motto -   *La fortune passe partout,* "Fortune makes
          way through everything"

- Rose of Kilravock -

Crest of the Chief

U.S. Society - Clan Rose Society

Blazon -   On a cap of maintenance
                 A harp azure

Motto -   Constant and true

- Ross of that Ilk -

Crest of the Chief

U.S. Society - Clan Ross Association of the United States, Inc.

Blazon -   *A hand holding a garland of juniper, all proper (The ancient crest was a garland of "laurel.")*

Motto -   *Spem successus alit,* "Success nourishes hope"

- Russell -

Ancient Crest

Blazon - *A dexter hand holding a skene proper and on the point thereof, a pair of balances, also proper*

Motto - *Virtus sine macula, "Virtue without stain"*

- Rutherford of that Ilk -

Ancient Crest

Blazon - *A martlet sable*

Motto - *Nec sorte nec fato,* "Neither by
chance, nor fate"

- Ruthven -

Crest of the Chief

Blazon -   *A ram's head couped sable, armed Or*

Motto -   *Deid Shaw,* "Deeds show" *or* "Actions show"

- Scott -

Crest of the Chief

U.S. Society - Clan Scott, U.S.A.

Blazon -   *A stagg trippant proper, attired and unguled Or*

Motto -   *Amo, "I love"*

- Scrymgeour -

Crest of the Chief

Blazon - *A lion's gamb erased in bend Or, holding a crooked sword or scimitar argent*

Motto - *Dissipate, "Scatter"*

- Sempill -

Crest of the Chief

Blazon - *Out of a ducal coronet*
A stag's head argent, attired with ten tynes azure,
collared with a prince's crown Or

Motto - *Keep Tryst,* "Keep the appointed meeting"

- Seton -

Ancient Crest

Blazon -   *A ducal coronet Or*
issuing therefrom a dragon vert spouting fire,
his wings elevated proper

Motto -   **Hazard yet forward, "There may be danger,**
but I will continue"

- Shaw of Tordarroch -

Crest of the Chief

U.S. Society - Clan Shaw Society

Blazon -   *A dexter cubit arm couped and holding a*
               dagger erect, all proper

Motto -   *Fide et fortitudine,* "By fidelity and fortitude"

- Sinclair -

Crest of the Chief

U.S. Society - Clan Sinclair Association (USA)

Blazon -   A cock proper, armed and beaked Or

Motto -   Commit thy work to God

- Skene of that Ilk -

Ancient Crest

U.S. Society - Clan Skene Association (USA)

Blazon -   *A dexter arm embowed issuing from a cloud, the hand holding a triumphal crown proper*

Motto -   *Virtutis regia merces,* "A palace the reward of bravery"

- Smith -

*Crest of the Clan Smith Society, Inc.
in the U.S.A.*

Blazon -   *A burning heart proper, winged argent*

Motto -   *Luceo non uro,* "I shine, not burn"

- Somerville -

Ancient Crest

Blazon -   *A dragon vert spouting fire proper, standing*
           on a wheel argent

Motto -   Fear God in life

- Spens -

Ancient Crest

Blazon - *A hart's head erased proper*

Motto - *Si deus quis contra,* "If God is for us, who is against us"

- Stuart of Bute -

Crest of the Chief

U.S. Society - The Clan Stewart Society in America, Inc.

Blazon -   *A demi-lion rampant gules, armed and*
langued azure

Motto -   *Nobilis est ira leonis,* "The wrath of the
lion is noble"

- Stewart of Appin -

Ancient Crest

Blazon -   *A unicorn's head argent, armed Or*

Motto -   *Quhidder will zie,* "Whither will ye,
                What will you do," *or*
                "What is your future"

- Stewart of Galloway -

Ancient Crest of
The Earls of Galloway

Blazon -   *A pelican in nest, vulning herself argent, winged or*

Motto -   *Virescit vulnere virtus,* **"Valour strengthens from a wound"**

- Stirling of Cadder -

Ancient Crest

Blazon -   *A swan's head and neck issuing out of a*
             ducal coronet proper

Motto -   *Gang forward, "Go forward"*

- Stirling of Cadder -

Crest of the Chief

Blazon -   *Issuing out of an antique coronet*
            A hart's head couped azure

Motto -   *Gang forward, "Go forward"*

- Strachan of Thornton -

Ancient Crest

Blazon -   *A demi-stag springing Or, holding in his mouth*
               a thistle proper

Motto -   *Non timeo sed caveo,* "I do not fear,
                           but am cautious"

- Sutherland -

Crest of the Chief

U.S. Society - Clan Sutherland Society of North America, Inc.

Blazon -   *A cat-a-mountain sejant rampant proper*

Motto -   *Sans peur, "Without fear"*

- Swinton of that Ilk -

Crest of the Chief

Blazon -   *A boar chained to an oak tree fructed, all proper*

Motto -   *J'espere,* "I hope"

- Trotter of Morton Hall -

Ancient Crest

Blazon - *A knight in armour proper, holding his courser argent, caparisoned gules*

Motto - *In promptu,* "In readiness"

- Turnbull -

Ancient Crest

Blazon -   A bull's head erased sable, armed vert

Motto -   I saved the King

- Tweedie -

Ancient Crest

Blazon - *A bull's head sable*

Motto - *Thol and think,* "Suffer and think" *or* "Wait and think"

- Urquhart of that Ilk -

Crest of the Chief

Blazon - Issuing from a crest coronet
A lady naked from the waist up proper, brandishing
in her dexter hand a sword azure, hilted and
pommelled gules, and in her sinister a palm sapling
vert

Motto - Meane weil, speake weil, doe weil, "Mean, speak
and do well"

- Wallace of that Ilk -

Crest of the Chief

U.S. Society - Clan Wallace Society (Worldwide)

Blazon -   *A dexter arm vambraced, the hand brandishing a sword, all proper*

Motto -   *Pro libertate,* "For liberty"

- Wardlaw -

Ancient Crest

Blazon -   *An estoile Or*

Motto -   *Familias firmat pietas*, "Religion
strengthens families"

- Wedderburn of that Ilk -

Crest of the Chief

Blazon -   *An eagle's head erased proper*

Motto -   *Non degener, "Not degenerated"*

- Weir -

Ancient Crest

Blazon - *On a chapeau gules, turned up ermine*
  A boar passant azure, bristled and unguled Or

Motto - *Vero nihil verius,* "Nothing truer than truth"

- Wemyss of that Ilk -

Crest of the Chief

Blazon -   *A swan proper*

Motto -   *Je pense*, "I think"

- Wood -

Ancient Crest

Blazon -   *A savage from the loins upwards, holding in his*
dexter hand a club erect, wreathed about the temples
and loins with laurel, all proper

Motto -   **Defend**

- Young -

Ancient Crest as borne by the Clan Young
of North America

Blazon -   *A lion issuing out of a wreath gules, holding
a sword in pale proper*

Motto -   *Robore prudentia præstat,* "Prudence excels
strength"

GLOSSARY PERTAINING TO THE CRESTS
AND SYMBOLIC MEANINGS OF DEVICES

Although certain symbolic meanings have been attached to the myriad devices of heraldry throughout the centuries, it does not necessarily follow that a particular device was granted to an individual with this symbolism in mind. Rather than representing a symbolic meaning, a device might pertain to the name of an individual. For instance, the arms that are known as *canting arms* are composed of devices alluding to the name of the bearer, such as the cocks (roosters) in the arms and crest of Cockburn and the fraise (strawberries) in the ancient arms of Lord Fraser of Muchalls. Arms such as these have been used most frequently throughout the course of heraldic history and are intended to suggest pictorially, rather than symbolically, the name of the armiger (one who bears a coat of arms). However, I consider it to be of interest, if not of importance, to include this glossary of terms and meanings as an adjunct to this book of crests.

A A A

ANCHOR	Represents hope.
ANTIQUE CROWN	(or EASTERN CROWN) Gold rim with five pointed rays showing.
ARM IN ARMOUR	Represents a person with qualities of leadership.
ARM, NAKED	Symbolizes an industrious person.
ARMED	Refers to the tinctures of claws or talons, and sometimes beaks, tusks or horns.
ARROW	Symbolizes readiness (for battle).

251

B B B

BALANCE	A pair of ancient beam scales.
BATON	Token of authority.
BATTLE AXE	The symbol of the execution of military duty.
BEAR	Symbolizes strength, cunning, and protection toward one's own kin.
BEE	The symbol of efficient industry.
BOAR	Wild boar. Symbol of bravery; one who fights to the death.
BOAR'S HEAD	A symbol of hospitality.
BOW	Usually shown with an arrow ready for flight. Symbolizes readiness (for battle).
BRANDISH	Not often used in heraldry but depending on the artist, it can mean either, "holding a weapon upright, as if ready to use it," or "waving the weapon above the head."
BULL	Represents valour, bravery, generosity. The horns represent strength and fortitude.

C C C

CAMEL	Represents patience and perseverance.
CASTLE	(or TOWER) Symbol of safety.
CAT-A-MOUNTAIN	(or CAT) represents liberty, vigilance and courage.
CHAPEAU	(or CAP OF MAINTENANCE) Made of velvet and ermine, it is granted to British peers and Scottish feudal barons.
CLOSE	Describes a bird with its wings closed against its body.
COCK	Symbol of courage and perseverance; badge of a hero.

CORONET, DUCAL	(or CREST CORONET) A gold coronet of four strawberry leaves, three showing.
CORONET, PRINCE'S	Coronet of the sovereign sons.
COUPED	Referring to heads and bodily extremities, cut off cleanly, as if with a guillotine.
CRANE	See Stork.
CRESCENT	Symbol of a person who has been honoured by his sovereign.
CREST BADGE	The badge worn by the clansman, comprising the crest of the chief encircled by a strap with which he attaches the badge to his tunic, and upon the strap is written the motto of the chief.
CREST CORONET	See Coronet, Ducal.
CREST WREATH	See Torse.
CROSS PATTEE- FITCHEE	A cross of three broad arms tapering to the centre, the lower arm tapering to a point at the base.
CROSS CROSSLET- FITCHEE	A cross crossed at three arms and pointed at the bottom. All crosses bear some sort of religious significance.
CROWN, IMPERIAL	The royal crown, as worn by a king or emperor.
CROWN, TRIUMPHAL	(or GARLAND) A wreath of laurel awarded by an army to its victorious leader.
CUBIT	A cubit arm means the forearm; below the elbow.
CUTLASS	Sword with broad curved blade, used by sailors.
CYPRESS	Symbolic of death and eternal life thereafter.

253

D D D

DAGGER	A short sword.
DART	An arrow. Symbolizes readiness (for battle).
DEMI	Prefix to describe the upper half; from waist up.
DEXTER	Pertaining to the right hand, or "on the right of" (on the left as you view it).
DEVICE	In heraldry, any singular part of the coat of arms. The shield, helmet, crest, crest wreath, motto, etc. Also, any individual part of the design upon the shield, e.g. a star, a cross, a dragon; all devices.
DOLPHIN	Unlike the living creature, a heraldic dolphin bears scales and is brightly coloured, green and scarlet when blazoned "proper." Said to represent swiftness, diligence and love.
DRAGON	Mythical beast, representing valour and protection.
DUCAL CORONET	See Coronet, Ducal.

E E E

EAGLE	Signifies a person of deeds and of noble nature, strength, bravery and alertness. The wings "displayed" symbolize protection and when depicted with two heads, the eagle represents the conjoining of two forces.
ERASED	Refers to the head or a bodily extremity as if torn from the body, leaving jagged edges.
ESCALLOP	(or SCALLOP SHELL) Symbol of the traveller to far places, also the symbol of a victorious naval commander.
ESTOILE	A star with six wavy points. Symbol of celestial goodness. Denotes a noble personage.

254

F F F

FALCON	See Hawk.
FETTERLOCK	A lock used to hobble horses. Symbol of victory.
FLEUR DE LIS	Golden lily and floral badge of France. Also mark of the sixth son (see Marks of difference).
FRAME SAW	A saw stretched within a square frame for rigidity.

G G G

GAMB	The foreleg of a beast.
GLOBE	The terrestrial globe (Earth), unless otherwise blazoned.
GOAT	Symbolizes one who wins through politics rather than war.
GOOSE, SOLAN	The gannet. Symbolizes resourcefulness.
GRIFFIN	(or GRYPHON). A mythical monster which, like the dragon, represents valour and bravery.

H H H

HAND	Always dexter unless otherwise blazoned. Represents sincerity, faith and justice.
HARP	Signifies a well composed person of tempered judgement. A symbol of contemplation.
HART	A male deer. See Stag.
HAWK	(or falcon). Represents one who does not rest until he achieves his objective.
HEART, FLAMING	Symbolizes intense, burning affection.
HEART, HUMAN	Symbol for charity and sincerity.

255

HERALDIC TIGER	Mythical beast. It has no stripes and is somewhere between a lion and a dragon.
HIND	Female deer. Symbol of peace and harmony.
HOLLY	Symbol of truth.
HORSE	Symbolizes readiness for all events.
HORSESHOE	Symbol of good luck and safeguard against evil spirits.

I I I

IMPERIAL CROWN	The royal crown; symbol of sovereign authority.

L L L

LADY	Wife of a noble. A device often used in coat armor, apparently of no other significance than aesthetics.
LANGUED	Refers to the tongue, when of a different tincture to the body.
LAUREL	Symbolizes peace and/or triumph.
LIGHTNING BOLT	Symbol of swiftness and power.
LION	The symbol of dauntless courage.
LIVERIES	The livery colours were originally the colours of the clothing in which a Noble clad his servants, often based on the main metal and colour of his arms. From about the beginning of the seventeenth century, armorial crests were usually granted "on a wreath of the colours" or "on a wreath of the liveries." To this day, the wreath below the crest is tinctured of the main metal and colour of the shield.
LOCHABER AXE	Type of battle axe.
LOCK	See Fetterlock.

M M M

MARKS OF DIFFERENCE
(cadency marks) The practice of using a symbol to difference the arms of a son from those of his father. See Crescent, Mullet, Martlet, Fleur de Lis and Rose.

MARTLET
Heraldic representation of the swallow, without feet or legs. Mark of the fourth son (see Marks of difference).

MERMAID
The body of a woman and tail of a fish. Usually depicted with mirror and comb. Symbol of eloquence.

MILL-RIND
The iron centrepiece of a mill stone; probably alludes to a miller.

MOOR
(BLACKAMOOR or NEGRO). Originally, a Moor was drawn with Arabic features, but is more usually drawn as negroid. Dating back to the Holy Crusades, when it was considered an honour to take a Moor's head.

MOUNT
(GRASSY HILLOCK). No particular heraldic significance; possibly a symbol of safety and protection, as is the rock.

MULLET
A star of five points. Represents in the bearer, divine quality from above. Mark of the third son (see Marks of difference).

N N N

NEGRO
Refers to conflicts with Moors and Saracens during the Holy Crusades. See Moor.

O O O

OAK TREE
(OAK BUSH). Symbol of great age and strength. When blazoned as fructed (with fruit), the tree is bearing acorns and symbolizes continuous growth and fertility.

257

OSTRICH	Symbol of willing obedience and serenity.
OTTER	Furry, aquatic fish-eating mammal. Symbolizes the individual who lives life to the fullest measure.

P P P

PARROT	No particular heraldic significance. When blazoned "proper," it is shown with green body, red beak and feet.
PASSION NAIL	A symbol of suffering by the original bearer of arms.
PEACOCK	Represents beauty, power and knowledge.
PELICAN	Usually depicted vulning herself (wounding her breast) to feed her young. Represents self-sacrifice and a person of charitable nature.
PHEON	(ARROW HEAD). As with the arrow, symbolizes readiness for battle.
POLE AXE	A type of battle axe.
PORTCULLIS	Fortified gate hung at the entrance to castles. Symbol of protection in an emergency.
PROPER	[abbrev. "ppr."] Used to describe any device in a coat of arms when displayed in its natural colours. The description of the device always precedes the colour: e.g. "an oak tree fructed proper."

R R R

RAINBOW	Representing good times after bad.
RAM	The leader. Represents authority.
RATCH-HOUND	A small beagle-type hound. Symbolizes loyalty, courage, and vigilance.
RAVEN	Symbol of divine providence.

ROCK	Symbol of safety and protection; a refuge.
ROSE	The mark of the seventh son (see Marks of difference). The white rose of York superimposed on the centre of the red rose of Lancaster is the floral badge of England; also called the Tudor rose.
ROSE, RED	Symbol of grace and beauty.
ROSE, WHITE	Symbol of faith and love.

S S S

SALAMANDER	(Ancient). Imaginary beast, resembling a wingless dragon engulfed in flame. Symbol of protection.
SALAMANDER	(Modern). Depicted as a lizard engulfed in flames.
SALTIRE	A diagonal cross (cross of Saint Andrew).
SAVAGE	(Saracen, wildman, woodman, green man). Usually depicted as a forest dweller dressed in leaves and carrying a club.
SCIMITAR	Oriental curved sword, broadened at the point.
SERPENT/SNAKE	Ancient symbol of wisdom.
SHEAF	(Of arrows). Unless otherwise blazoned: three arrows, banded and tied.
SHIP	Usually an ancient sailing ship or lymphad. Pertains to ancient sea voyages.
SHIP, DISMASTED	Represents a disaster at sea.
SINISTER	Pertaining to the left hand, or "on the left side of." (On the right as you view it.)
SOLAN GOOSE	See goose.
SPEAR	(TILTING LANCE). Symbolizes the honourable warrior, the valiant knight.

SPUR	A gold spur is that of a knight, silver for an esquire. Symbolizes preparedness; always ready for action.
SPUR ROWEL	The spiked star of the spur.
STAG	Male (red) deer. One who will not fight unless severely provoked. Symbol of peace and harmony, the antlers represent strength and fortitude.
STAR	Usually blazoned as a mullet or estoile. When described as a star, the number of points or "rays" is mentioned.
STORK	In heraldry, the stork and crane are usually depicted as the same bird. The symbol of close parental bond. Also symbolizes vigilance if holding a rock; if he goes to sleep, he drops the rock and wakes.
STRAWBERRIES	(FRAISES; French). Rarely used in heraldry. Fraise usually refers to the cinquefoil, the strawberry blossom of five petals, but occasionally it refers to the fruit.
SUN	(In splendour). Symbol of glory and splendour; fountain of life.
SUNFLOWER	Rarely used in heraldry. Large flower which follows the sun across the sky.
SWAN	Symbol of poetic harmony and learning.
SWORD	Symbolizes justice and honour.

T T T

TARGE	A circular shield with a boss in the centre.
THISTLE	Floral badge of Scotland. Usually depicted in stylized form.
THUNDERBOLT	From ancient mythology, a flaming winged column with four bolts of lightning radiating in saltire from the centre.

TORSE	(CREST WREATH). The double, twisted silken scarves laid on the helmet and encircling the crest.
TOTEM	The effigy of a natural animate being, usually an animal or bird, used by North American Indians as a symbol of tribal clan or kinship. When these effigies are carved into or hung upon an upright pole, this is known as a totem pole.
TOWER	Symbol of safety and grandeur.
TREE TRUNK	(Sprouting). Usually oak. Symbolic of new life sprouting from old.
TRIUMPHAL CROWN	(Garland). A wreath of laurel leaves and berries, worn by triumphant Roman emperors as a symbol of victory and peace.

U U U

UNGULED	Referring to hoofs of animals when of a different tincture to the body.
UNICORN	Mythological horse-like creature with single horn radiating from its forehead. Symbol of extreme courage.

V V V

VAMBRACED	Vambrace is armour worn on the arm, and "vambraced" refers to the arm fully clad in armour.
VINE TREE	(Grape vine). Symbolic of strong and lasting friendship.

W W W

WHEEL	Symbol of fortune.
WINGS	Symbolize swiftness and protection.

WOLF	Represents reward from perseverance and hard industry.
WYVERN	A dragon with only two legs and an "armed" tail of a serpent. Represents valour and protection.

HERALDIC TINCTURES
AND THEIR SYMBOLIC MEANINGS

METALS
OR	GOLD	Symbolizes generosity and elevation of mind.
ARGENT	SILVER	Symbolizes peace and sincerity.

COLOURS
GULES	RED	Represents the warrior, brave and strong but generous and just; the martyr's colour.
AZURE	BLUE	Symbolizes truth and loyalty.
VERT	GREEN	Symbolizes hope, joy and love.
SABLE	BLACK	Symbolizes constancy or grief.

FUR
ERMINE	WHITE WITH BLACK SPOTS - Winter fur of the weasel; all white with a black tipped tail.

PROPER
(Abbreviated "ppr.") Refers to a device when displayed in its natural colour: e.g. "an oak tree fructed proper" means "an oak tree bearing acorns in their natural colours."

Heraldic Tinctures

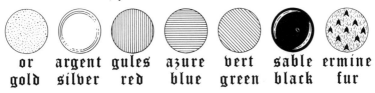

or	argent	gules	azure	vert	sable	ermine
gold	silver	red	blue	green	black	fur

Hatching: lines and dots used to represent tinctures